Robert Williams Buchanan

The Piper of Hamelin

A Fantastic Opera in Two Acts

Robert Williams Buchanan

The Piper of Hamelin
A Fantastic Opera in Two Acts

ISBN/EAN: 9783337397579

Printed in Europe, USA, Canada, Australia, Japan

Cover: Foto ©Thomas Meinert / pixelio.de

More available books at **www.hansebooks.com**

THE
PIPER OF HAMELIN.

ℨantastic Ꙩpera

IN TWO ACTS

By ROBERT BUCHANAN.

WITH ILLUSTRATIONS

BY

HUGH THOMSON.

LONDON:

PRINTED AT THE CHISWICK PRESS,

1893.

*** The Legend of the Pied Piper appears in the folk-lore of several countries, and has been localized even in England, on the banks of the Solent. It has been thought advisable, however, to keep the scene of the present opera in Germany. While the plot of the first act follows to a great extent the well-known legend versified by Browning, the scheme of the second act, including the restoration of the children, is entirely new and original.

R. B.

CHARACTERS.

The Burgomaster of Hamelin.
Conrad the Cooper.
Citizen Sauerkraut.
Citizen.
Other Citizens.
The Town Crier.
The Pied Piper.

Chorus of Citizens, Handicraftsmen, etc.

Liza, the Burgomaster's Daughter.
Martha, his Servant.
Hans, a little lame Boy.
Deborah Meerschaum.
An old Woman.
A Widow.

Chorus of Market-girls and of Children.

————

Act I.—The Market-Place of Hamelin, in Brunswick.
Act II.—Mountain-side near the Town.

————

Time—Fifteenth century.

THE PIPER OF HAMELIN.

ACT I.

SCENE. *The Market-place of Hamelin, with view of Clock Tower and Bridge. Very quaint, old-fashioned town. Up stage, R., the Bridge, with river winding beneath it, and beyond, on cloth, the town on a hill, with an old-fashioned church. Down L., the Town-hall, looking on Market-place. Stalls covered with wares of all kinds extend right up to Bridge. Market girls and men discovered selling flowers, fish, pipes, etc.*

Chorus.

WHO'LL buy ? who'll buy ?
Here's ware for all wishes,
Fresh capons, fishes,
To boil or fry !
New plates, new dishes.
Come buy ! come buy !

A Voice. Here's a flower for the lady !
A Voice. And a coral for the baby !

7

A Voice. And a pipe for the Herr Papa!
Chorus. And a pipe for the Herr Papa!

Come buy! come buy!
Here's ware of all prices,
Of all devices,
For low and high.
Here's whatever nice is!
Come buy! come buy!

A Voice. Here's a ring for the lady!
A Voice. And a cradle for the baby!
A Voice. And a pipe for the Herr Papa!
A Voice. And a pipe for the Herr Papa!

Enter CONRAD.

(*Recitative.*)

Con. How dreary seem the many cries around me!
I have search'd from street to street and cannot find her.
There by the church my darling vow'd to meet me,
For hours I've waited, and alas! she lingers.
Yonder her door is—if I dared but venture,
Softly I'd knock, and tell her I await her!
But ah! I'm poor, and she's the great Mayor's
daughter,
And much I fear her purse-proud father's anger.

Ballad.

Sweet Star up yonder,
O'er which I ponder,
Made ever fonder

8

As fleet hours fly ;
Though far above me,
Your light doth move me,
For ah ! you love me,
Though set so high !

Chorus. (*Pianissimo.*) Come buy ! come buy !

Con. Ah yes, you love me,
Though set so high!

Chorus. Come buy !
A Girl. Here's a ring for the lady!
All. Come buy !
A Girl. And a cradle for the baby !
Chorus. Come buy !
A Man. And a pipe for the Herr Papa !
Chorus of Men. Ha, ha ! Ha, ha !
Con. (*Petulantly.*) But I'm *not* a Herr Papa !
Chorus. (*Laughing.*) Ha, ha !
He's not a Herr Papa !

Enter MARTHA, *with market basket.*

Con. Ah, Martha, good morning !
Mar. Good morning, Master Conrad.
Con. Marketing, eh ?
Mar. Getting in provision for the old cormorant, my master. Dear, dear, what an appetite he has ! Capons, carrots, turnips, fish—but there, all's fish that comes to his gobble ! I wish it would choke him, I do, indeed !

9 B

Con. Isn't he a good master ?

Mar. Good ? I'd as lief serve the—hem ! It isn't for myself I care, though flesh and blood couldn't stand such treatment long, but I grieve for the sweet Fraulein, my mistress. You know what a life he leads her ?

Con. I do indeed !

Mar. Grudges her the very clothes she wears—the very morsel she eats.

Con. Well, tell her——

Mar. Yes ?

Con. Tell her—by the bye, where is he now ?

Mar. The Mayor ? Yonder in the Town-hall, discussing the great plague of rats with which the town is infested. You see, it all comes through his stinginess. If he had employed a proper rat-killer at first, at a proper price, they would have been exterminated ; but now they're grown to such a pest, that I fear they'll eat us out of house and home.

Con. (*Up, looking off.*) Liza ! . . . There she is, looking as bright and happy as if there were no trouble in the world !

[*Signals to* Martha *and moves behind house* L., *as* Liza *enters over bridge.*

Song, " *Liza* " (*with obligato violin accompaniment*).

I.

A youth there was who loved a little maiden,
    And whisper'd " Sweet, how dear thou art to me ! "
She laugh'd, and ran away into the greenwood,
    Where birds were singing loud from every tree.

10

"Now May is near!" they sang so clear,
    "And May's the merry time of wooing!"
The simple maiden blush'd to hear,
    But hoped—the youth was still pursuing!
Her cheeks like roses were, her eyes
The same soft blue as the blue skies.
She was very simple, very simple, very simple,
        O so simple!
And yet within her heart began to sound
The same glad song the birds were singing round!
Though she was but a simple country maiden
    She loved that song, "How dear thou art to me!"
And she beckon'd to her lover through the green-
        wood,
    While the birds were singing loud on every tree.

II.

The happy youth came running to the maiden,
    And kiss'd her on the lips with kisses three!
She hid her blushing face upon his bosom,
    And who in all the world was glad as he?
Afar and near the birds sang clear,
    "May is the merry time of wooing!"
The happy lovers laugh'd to hear,
    And kiss'd again, their bliss renewing.
They were very simple, very simple, very simple,
        O so simple!
And yet the wisest man alive that day
Could not be wiser in love's ways than they.

Though she was but a simple country maiden,
　　And he a simple swain of low degree,
They understood the message of the May-time,
　　Which the birds were singing loud from every
　　　　tree !

Con. Liza !

Liza. Conrad ! How you frightened me ! I thought——

Con. (*Laughing.*) That one of those precious rats had pounced upon you ? There, don't be afraid, *I* shan't eat you !　　　　[*Cries off.* Children *run in.*

Liza. What is it, little ones ?

A Little Girl. The rats ! the rats ! They came out of their holes while we were at school, and they're eating up all the books.

Enter HANS, *a little lame boy with crutch.*

Hans. Help ! help ! (*Runs* to LIZA.) O Liza, I'm so frightened !

Liza. At what, dear ?　　　[Children *surround them.*

Hans. The rats ! They've stolen my dinner, and I thought they would have eaten *me*, for though I fought them with my crutch, they didn't mind.

Liza. You're safe here, at any rate. (*Aside to* CONRAD.) Poor little fellow, his mother is dead, and his father has married again. You know what *that* means !

" I was sitting alone at the top of the stair."

Hans. (*Nestling to and looking up at* LIZA.) I'm not afraid *now*, Liza!

Liza. That's right. Now tell us how it all happened!

Rat-a-pat Song. HANS, LIZA *and* Chorus.

Hans. I was sitting alone at the top of the stair,
    Eating my dinner of dry, black bread,
Stepmother had whipt me and sent me there,
    Because I was ugly and bad, she said.
And I said my prayers, for I felt afraid
    Of the great black lonely place,
And I thought as I pray'd that I saw in the shade
    My own dear mother's face.
Liza. (*Smoothing his hair.*) Poor child! poor child!
Hans. (*Mysteriously.*) Then I heard a sound
Upstairs, downstairs, and all around,
Rat-a-pat! . . . . rat-a-pat! . . . .
And I saw from the corner where I sat
The rats were running this way and that,
With a rat-a-pat, and a rat-a-pat!
And some were lean and some were fat,
And they show'd their teeth and seem'd to say,
"We'll make a meal of this boy to-day."
And then one great big monster rat
Came climbing up to where I sat,
With a rat-a-pat and a rat-a-pat,
    And I scream'd, and ran away!
    [Chorus *repeat.* Children *flock together terrified.*

13

Conrad, recitative.

Bolder and bolder are the rascals growing,
  Soon in broad day they'll throng and overpower us,
Where they will stop their ravage, there's no knowing,
  Unless some help comes quickly, they'll devour us.
       [*A scream up stage.* Women *run down.*

Liza.   What's that? what's that?
Children. A rat! a rat!
         See where he crawls
         Among the stalls!
   [Women *scream and gather up their petticoats in
    horror.*
Children. (*Retreating.*) Look, there's another,
         His great big brother!
         A monster rat,
         As big as a cat!
Con. Where is he, where?
Men and Girls. Look *there!*   [Girls *scream.*

Conrad, recitative.

Such impudence is not to be endured!
  In broad daylight—the very devil's in it!
Keep back, and you shall see the rascal skewer'd
  Upon my glittering sword's point in a minute!
     Take that! and that! [*Thrusting under stalls.*

Chorus.   He has kill'd the rat.
Con.   Yes, friends, 'tis done,
         His race is run.

14

Men.	Now kill the other,
	His great big brother.
Con.	Take that! and that!
Men.	He has done it pat!
All.	He has kill'd the rat!

Con. (*To* LIZA.) Come, have no fear—

They're here!

[*Showing rats on sword. General murmurs of horror.*

Liza. Horrible monsters!

Con. Courage, Liza, dearest!
I will protect thee from the swarms thou fearest.
Trust to my prowess, calm this wild pulsation!

Crier. (*Without.*) Room for the Mayor—the Mayor
and Corporation!

[*Murmurs without. Bells ring, crowd gathers up,
and during following scene many of the stalls
are cleared and carried off, clearing the stage.*

Chatter-Chorus.

Why this clatter? what's the matter?
  Why that loud vociferation?
Something stirring is occurring
  To the Mayor and Corporation.
Heaven defend us! some stupendous
  Terror in the Town-hall's found them!
From some shocking sight they're flocking,
  Casting frighten'd looks around them!

Enter Town Crier, *on steps of Town-hall.*

Crier. Good people all, of every occupation,
Make room there for the Mayor and Corporation !

Enter, from Town-hall, Mayor *and* Aldermen.

Chorus.

Why this clatter ? what's the matter ?
Pray what means this acclamation ?
Cease your chatter ! cease your chatter !
How his heart goes patter patter !——
He is driven to desperation.

Song. The Mayor.

Alas ! alas ! for Hamelin city,
Will no one help us and take pity ?
By a pest more dire than snake or locust,
We're driven distracted and hocus-pocus'd ;
The rats, the rats, are coming to win
The beautiful city of Hamelin.
            Chorus. The rats, etc.

As there in council we sat inditing
Civic matters of draining and lighting,
Judging causes, arranging *your* rates,
Discussing problems of tithes and poor rates,
The rats, the rats, came swarming in,
Affrighting us burghers of Hamelin.
            Chorus. The rats, etc.

16

"The rats, the rats, came swarming in,
Affrighting us burghers of Hamelin."

Without so much as a word of warning,
All our arts to appal them scorning !
Though ink and paper we scatter'd at them,
Nothing would fright them off, Od rat them !
They took possession, despite our skin,
Of the very Town-hall of Hamelin.
Chorus. They took, etc.

We call'd the clergy with book and candle,
To curse the vermin and end the scandal,
They frighten'd the clergy and overpower'd them,
They seized the candles, and they devour'd them,
They gnaw'd the principal parson's shin,
These terrible rats of Hamelin.
Chorus. They gnaw'd, etc.

Alas ! alas ! for Hamelin city,
Doom'd to be eaten, the more's the pity !
By a pest more dire than snake or locust,
Your Mayor's distracted and hocus-pocus'd.
The rats, the rats, are coming to win,
The beautiful town of Hamelin.
Chorus. The rats, the rats, etc.

Chatter-Chorus.

Sad disaster ! thicker, faster,
  To destroy men's occupation,
Come the ermine-eating vermin,
  Frighting Mayor and Corporation.
Heaven defend us ! this tremendous
  Plague will end in desperation.

17   c

Mayor. (*Loudly and angrily.*) Stop that ringing from
   the steeple !
  Clear the square of all the people !
  Here'll we'll sit in consultation.
Chorus. Here they'll sit in consultation.
Crier.   Clear the square !
   Obey the Mayor !
[*During following, trestle-table is brought out, and
 forms for the* Aldermen *to sit on.*

Chorus of Girls. Clear the square,
   Well I declare !
Crier.   Obey the Mayor !

(*Ensemble.*)

Mayor and Council.   *Citizens.*   *Conrad and Liza.*

We're the Mayor and Corporation,   They're the Mayor
We must try in consultation,   and Corporation,
To devise some lawful measures   etc.
How to save our lives and treasures.
Our provisions are decreasing
Through this pest of rats unceasing :
Oil and tallow, eggs and bacon,
Fowl, fish, flesh, have all been taken ;
When the city's stores are eaten,
We shall be completely beaten—
Then, perchance (O sad reflection !)
They'll conclude their fierce refection
With a horrid cold collation
Of the Mayor and Corporation !
18

Crier. Clear the square !

[*Flourish. Table and forms having been brought out, the* MAYOR, *the* TOWN CLERK, *and others, sit pompously.* CRIER *stands attending.*

Mayor. Bring me the town records.

[CLERK *brings an enormous volume half eaten away.*

Clerk. Please, your worship, that's all that's left of them !

Crier. O—yes, that's all that's left of them !

Mayor. Silence, idiot !

Crier. Silence, id . . . (*correcting himself*). Beg pardon, your worship !

Mayor. (*Examining book.*) You see, gentlemen, even the town records are nearly eaten away—through no fault of mine. Clerk, produce the old bell-rope ! (*Rope produced.*) Gnawed, you see, into pieces. If we had not had the foresight to provide a new rope, the great bell would have come down—through no fault of mine.

Sauerkraut. No fault of yours ! Why, these rats have destroyed the boots in my shop.

1st Citizen. And all the dry goods in my store ! Unless something is done there won't be a piece of toffee left in the town.

All. Shame ! Shame !

Mayor. Gentlemen, I agree with all you say. In the whole course of my civic experience I have never encountered so grave a calamity. But it arises, as I have explained, through no fault of mine. Has anyone anything to suggest ?

19

Crier. Oh yes! oh yes! Has anyone anything to suggest?

Sauerkraut. Well, I'm a plain man——

Mayor. Stop a minute, Brother Sauerkraut! Be good enough to address your observations to the Mayor and the Chair.

Sauerkraut. Oh, all right! As I was saying——

Mayor. Address your remarks to *me*, sir!

Crier. Oh yes! oh yes! Address your remarks to me.

Sauerkraut. I say I'm a plain man——

Mayor. You are a very plain man—through no fault of mine. Ha! ha! But be careful; as the Mayor of this town——

1st Citizen. Oh, bother him!

All. Yes, bother the Mayor!

Mayor. Gentlemen, am I right in supposing that observation was addressed to me?

Sauerkraut. Certainly; you've bothered us long enough, why shouldn't we bother you?

1st Citizen. If you put that motion I'll second it.

All. Hear! hear!

Mayor. Gentlemen, you astound me! I should be sorry to think I'd lost your confidence.

Sauerkraut. You haven't.

Mayor. Ah!

Sauerkraut. You couldn't lose what you never possessed.

Mayor. I regret to see, gentlemen, that you underrate my value.

" Here we'll sit in consultation."

Sauerkraut. No, we don't.

Mayor. Ah!

Sauerkraut. We can't underrate what never existed.

1st Citizen. Bravo, Sauerkraut!

Mayor. Enough; the meeting is dismissed. Crier, dismiss the meeting.

Crier. Oh yes! oh yes!

Sauerkraut. But I say, Oh no! oh no! Citizens, the hour has come to strike a blow for freedom!

Mayor. What, a blow?

Sauerkraut. Sit down! The faĉt of the matter is, we owe our misfortunes to you. Trade has dwindled and declined.

Mayor. Through no fault of mine.

Sauerkraut. I beg your pardon; there were no taxes till you turned them into turtle. Our goods were free of duty till you negleĉted yours. False economy!

1st Citizen. Gluttonous gastronomy!

Sauerkraut. Muddling!

1st Citizen. And fuddling!

Sauerkraut. Have brought us to this pass. In order to save a few guilders, which you have wasted in guzzling, you dismissed Hans Breitman, the town rat-catcher, and when he went our troubles began—this plague of rats.

Mayor. I admit there is a rat or two.

Sauerkraut. A rat or two! the place swarms with them! And the long and the short of it is that either you consent to sign this proclamation or forthwith cease to be Mayor of Hamelin.

Mayor. Gentlemen, you'll excuse me, but I've an important appointment.

Sauerkraut. That won't do for us! Either sign or resign. Crier, read the proclamation.

Crier. Oh yes! oh yes! I, the Mayor of Hamelin, offer a reward of a thousand guilders to whosoever shall rid the town of the plague of rats that now infests our city.

Sauerkraut. Your signature.

Mayor. Never!

Sauerkraut. Then by the unanimous decree of the Corporation——

Mayor. I don't care a fig for the Corporation; I've an excellent corporation of my own.

Sauerkraut (and the others threaten him). What!

Mayor. Give me a pen.

[*He signs, and the* CRIER *goes out shouting the proclamation, the crowd following with cheers.*

Mayor. (*Alone.*) And this is civic gratitude. I could cry with vexation. So humiliating; and before all the servants too. But Frederick Schofferganger will be a match for them yet. Where are they going to find their ratcatcher? and where is the ratcatcher going to find his thousand guilders? Not in this part of the town, I think. (*Slaps his pocket.*) But it's awkward. However, I'll cool my head under the town pump and think it out. Hey, what's this?

[*Goes up, then pauses, watching, as enter* CONRAD *and* LIZA.

Con. At last, darling, we are alone.

22

Liza. But I still feel terribly frightened.

Con. There is no occasion. If the worst comes to the worst we will fly together.

Liza. But whither ?

Con. Anywhere—where the rats cannot follow us.

Liza. But my father ?

Con. Young birds leave the nest—so do young maidens. Leave the old fellow to his money-bags ; he'll never miss you.

Mayor. (*Up.*) What's this I hear ?

Duet.

I.

Con. When its wings are grown the young thrush
    flies.
Both. Sing hey ! the sweet spring weather.
Con. It seeks its mate 'neath the sunny skies,
    And they make their home together.
Both. They build their nest together.
Con. They build their nest, and they warble free,
  On the leafy bough of the greenwood tree,
  "I love my love, and my love loves me !"
  They sing in the sun together.   [*Repeat.*

II.

Con. The young maid flies from the parent nest.
Both. Sing hey ! the wind and the weather.
Con. She chooses the partner she loves the best,
    And for others cares not a feather.

23

The lover wooeth as *I* woo *thee*,
The young maid smiles and they both fly free,
" I love my love, and my love loves me ! "
They sing in the sun together.   [*Repeat*.

Mayor. (*Coming down.*) Hem! when you have *quite*
finished.

Liza. My father !

Con. The Mayor !

Mayor. Sorry to interrupt you, I am sure.   May I
ask you your name ?

Con. Conrad.

Mayor. Who and what are you ?

Con. Conrad the Cooper ; a simple handicrafts-
man, of this town.

Liza. O, father, don't be angry !   He loves me !

Mayor. Very pretty !   And you——

Liza. And I love *him*.   Ah, yes !

Mayor. Stop !   No embracing in my presence.
Young man, if I understand you, you are a pauper ?

Liza. No, no !

Con. I am poor, it is true.

Mayor. Poor but virtuous, I suppose.   Oh yes, we
have heard all that before ; so off with you to your
hoops and staves, and never dare to address my
daughter again !

Liza. Oh no, no !   Father, don't drive him away.

Mayor. If he doesn't go at once, I'll send for the
watch and have him locked up in the town prison.

Con. What is my offence ?   That I love your

'I'll cool my head under the Town Pump:'

" I'll cool my head under the town pump and think it out ! "

daughter is true; that I am not her equal in rank is
also true; but she has overlooked the disparity between
us, and I will not give her up without a struggle.

Mayor. You won't, eh?

Con. Certainly not.

Mayor. You defy me?

Con. If you put it that way, yes.

Mayor. And you, Liza?

Liza. Father, I implore you.

Mayor. Home, at once, or I'll cut you off without a
groschen. 			[*Laughter and cries off.*

Mayor. What sounds are those?

Crier. (*Entering.*) So please your worship, the towns-
people following one who looks like a beggar or street
musician. 			[*Music off; then laughter.*

Mayor. What's that?

Crier. He is playing upon a pair of miserable bag-
pipes. Look, he comes this way.

> [*Music and jeers continued. Enter* Men *and*
> Women, *laughing, shouting, then the* PIPER.
> *He is a quaint looking figure in piebald
> costume, decorated with skins of moles, birds,
> rats, mice, snakes, etc., very ragged and wild.
> Hideous music People jeer.*

Mayor. (*Stopping his ears.*) Silence! Silence, I say!
Call the watch! How dare you make such an infernal
noise in the public streets! Who are you?

Crier. Oh yes! Who are you?

Piper. A poor wandering musician, at your service.

Mayor. A vagrant and a beggar, by your own con-

fession. I commit you as a public nuisance. Arrest
him! [*Movement.*

Piper. Stop a minute! I've come in answer to the
proclamation.

Mayor. Eh?

Piper. You offer a reward of a thousand guilders to
anyone who will relieve the town of its vermin.

Mayor. We do; but there——

Piper. I'm a musician by nature, and a vermin-
killer by profession. Say the word, and I'll do the job
for you.

Mayor. You! Pooh! [*All laugh.*

Piper. Yes, me!

Mayor. Fiddlededee! Pray how do you propose to
set about it?

Piper. I'll tell you. I'll charm anything under the
sun by my beautiful music.

[*Blows on pipes. Discordant music. All stop their
ears.*

Mayor. This is hideous. Away with him!

Piper. Stop! P'r'aps you don't know who I am.
Listen, and I'll tell you!

Song. "*The Piper.*"

Good people all, give heed to me, for I'm the Piper of
     Pipers,
I charm all things on land or sea, rats, mice, jackdaws,
     and vipers.

I've but to blow in my pipes—just so! [*Music, they stop their ears*]—and they'll follow the sound with pleasure :

Dogs and cats, bats, snakes and rats, will dance away to the measure.

As a Piper of fame they know my name in every town and nation !

My terms are low, for you must know, I delight in my occupation.

At Timbuctoo King Kalabaloo was plagued with huge Bluebottles—

They darken'd the street, they spoil'd the meat, they stuck in the people's throttles !

Buzz ! boom !
In every room
Coming and going,
Indoors and out,
They swarm'd about,
Buzz ! boom !
Fuzzing and buzzing and blowing.

During this the people are spell-bound, and have business of see-ing and catch-ing bluebottles. Chord, and the ballad is re-newed.

Well, I play'd a tune on my pipes, and soon the pest was exterminated ;

So I took my pay and I stroll'd away, much honour'd and decorated :

27

And I cross'd the sea to Tartaree with little procrastination,

And I found the Khan was a wretched man, for the
Daws were a sad vexation.

Daws !
Jenny-daws, jackdaws,
Grey daws, black daws,
Not a nook in the realm did lack
daws !
Wherever you went you heard
their caws,
They ate the corn and they left
the straws,
They wrangled and jangled with-
out a pause,
They swarm'd about with their
goblin jaws,
They darken'd the air, they defied
the laws,
With a fluent vociferation.
They had ravenous claws and teeth
like saws,
Everything nice went into their
maws,
From sugar and spice to hips and
haws,
Till nothing was left in the
nation !

*Daw music. People
gape, look up,
stop ears, etc.
End on chord
as before.*

28

Well, I play'd a tune on my pipes, and soon, to the
    joy of the starving people,
Of those birds unclean not one was seen on tree, or
    house, or steeple ;
And I sailed away into Indi-ay, with little procrastination,
And found the folk in a frightful way, for the Snakes
    were abomination.

                  Snakes !
        Hissing and crawling
        In a way appalling,
        From woods and brakes :
        Red snakes, green snakes,
        Fat snakes, lean snakes !
        Vipers and cobras
        All the unclean snakes !
        Rustling and creeping
        With venomous heads ;
        Coil'd up, and sleeping
        In cupboards, in beds !
With horrible stings and slimy
    eye-sockets,
Creeping up petticoats, crawling
    in pockets,
Strangling the babies, hissing, and
    clinging,
When least expected, upspringing
    and stinging,
Scattering death in a brace of shakes.
    Ugh ! SNAKES !

*Snake - business
among crowd.
Women cry,
and jump on
benches, etc.*

29

But I play'd a tune on my pipes and soon cobra and
  serpent and viper
Came wriggling out, and went dancing about, in the
  wake of the wondrous Piper.
And I led them away to an ocean bay, and play'd
  them into the water,
And there they were drown'd, and the shores around
  for leagues were black with the slaughter.

So now you know, though I'm poor and low, that I'm
  the Piper of Pipers.
I charm and slay, wherever I stray, rats, crickets, daws
  and vipers,
I've but to blow in my pipes—just so ! [*Blows, they stop
  their ears*]—and they follow the sound with
  pleasure,
Daws, dogs and rats, bats, snakes and cats, will dance
  away to the measure !

That's the sort of man I am.
 Mayor. Is it possible that you can help us ?
 Piper. (*Drily*.) What's your poison ?
 Mayor. Eh ?
 Piper. What are you plagued with ? Cats, dogs,
cobras, fleas, earwigs, beetles, locusts, bees, wasps,
hornets, moles, crocodiles, armadilloes, centipedes,
cockchafers, or daddy-longlegs ?
 Mayor. No, rats.
 All. Yes, rats !

Piper. Then it's lucky I came your way. I'm death on that kind of vermin.

Mayor. But *our* rats are not ordinary rats, they're a race of monsters.

Piper. So much the better. All rats are fond of music.

Mayor. (*Scornfully.*) Of *your* music?

Piper. Of mine particularly. Oh, rats have excellent taste, your worship, I assure you! What's the reward?

Mayor. A thousand golden guilders.

Piper. Pay the money, and it's done!

Mayor. Excuse me, good payers never pay beforehand.

Piper. Then sign a little agreement.

Mayor. What! (*Pompously*) I am the Mayor of Hamelin, and my word is my bond.

Piper. (*Doubtfully.*) I suppose I can trust your worship?

Mayor. On the honour of a magistrate!

Piper. Humph! Well, it's a bargain. I'll kill the rats.

All. He'll kill the rats

Mayor. When will you begin, fellow?

Piper. No time like the present.

Mayor. I'm afraid you'll find it a long job.

Piper. Oh dear, no—a bagatelle!

Song. *Piper and Chorus.*

Now, clear the way while I essay
   A charm of strange device !
With hands so bold I weave (behold !)
   A circle round me thrice.
Attend ! give heed, ye hideous breed,
Wherever ye creep and crawl and feed,
Attend ! appear !

Rats. (*Squeak off.*) We hear ! We hear !
Piper. I'll fix them in a trice.
All. He'll fix them in a trice !
Piper. First, to make the charm complete,
   Hear me your royal names repeat.

            Abracadabra !   [*Squeak.*
            Smellfungus !   [*Squeak.*
            Salamander !   [*Squeak.*
            Sanerteig !   [*Squeak.*
Hearken, hearken, one and all,
Ye kings of ratland, while I call.
Attend ! appear !   [*Loud squeaking off.*
Citizen. Oh, hark ! they hear !
Voices.   We hear !

Invocation. The Piper.

   Attend, ye rats !
Come from your nests in greasy vats,
Forsake your feasts of salted sprats,
Leave cheese to mice, and flesh to cats !

"Give ear, give ear! O rats, appear!
And follow, follow me!"

Where'er ye crawling be!
Give ear, give ear! O rats, appear!
And follow, follow me!

[*He goes up playing and stands on bridge. Wild
music. A great squealing and squeaking is
heard off,* L.

Chatter-Chorus (with rat music in orchestra).

Sight appalling! see them crawling
  Out of every door and dwelling;
Tails they're whisking, gladly frisking,
  Never pausing or rebelling.
Faster, thicker! quicker, quicker!
Wild and glad as men in liquor,
Cocking ears and twirling whiskers,
Ancient rats and gay young friskers,
Baby ratlings, he rats, she rats
Leading young and giving suction,
Everywhere we gaze we see rats
Trotting on to their destruction.

[*During above Chorus swarms of rats are seen to
cross stage and follow* PIPER *over the bridge.
People look on in wonder. All gradually disappear
except the* MAYOR.

Mayor. Thank heaven my weary burthen is up-
lifted. I should like to know what Mayor Bum-
melzug will say now. My office is safe for another
year.

[*Music. Wild squealing heard off. Then shouts
" Hurrah! "*

33   E

Enter CONRAD *with* LIZA.

Con. Hurrah ! I bring you good news—the rats are all destroyed !

Mayor. Destroyed ?

Con. Drowned in the river. The Piper stood on one side, they entered it on the other, and every one was drowned.

Mayor. Hurrah ! Ring the bells ! We'll have a civic banquet on the spot.

[*Bells ring joyfully.*

Enter Corporation.

Recitative.

Mayor. (*Pompously.*) Well, gentlemen, you see I've
    kept my promise.
The rats are totally exterminated ;
I hope you now regret your hasty language.

Citizens. Oh, yes, we now regret our hasty lan-
    guage.

Mayor. And all will join me at a civic banquet,
Which will be paid for by the public pocket.

Citizens. Good ! 'twill be paid for by the public
    pocket. [*Shake hands.*

Song. Mayor and Chorus.

Come, haste away, this very day,
    To celebrate with jollity
This happy news, which will excuse
    A little gay frivolity.

34

We'll gaily dine and end in wine
   The fears we felt so chillingly ;
The ratepayers will think it fine
   To pay the Piper willingly.
    Chorus. (*Chuckling.*) Ha, ha !
    They'll pay the Piper willingly !

As they are going off, enter PIPER.

Piper. (*Wiping brow.*) Well, it's all right, governor.
Mayor. (*Coldly.*) Ah ! How d'ye do !
Piper. I've done the job, your worship.
Mayor. What ! the rats !—
Piper. All drowned—exterminated.
Mayor. You are sure ? All dead ?
Piper. Every one.
Mayor. Can't come to life again ?
Piper. No. Dead as nails.
Mayor. Then I think I'll go to dinner. Come,
gentlemen.
   Piper. Stop !   [*Chord.*
Mayor. Eh ?
Piper. My little fee—the thousand guilders.
Mayor. Call to-morrow at the Town-hall.
Piper. I leave for Seringapatam this evening.
Mayor. Well, send in your little bill, and it shall be
attended to.
  Piper. Can't wait. Come, pay up !
Mayor. (*Aside.*) What do you say, gentlemen ? I
suppose the man has earned his money ?

Sauerkraut. That's *your* affair.

Citizens. Of course!

Mayor. Mine? It's yours also. He will be paid out of the public treasury.

Sauerkraut. Certainly not.

Citizens. Certainly not.

Sauerkraut. It was your bargain; pay the man, and let him go.

Mayor. I shall do nothing of the sort. It is preposterous!

Piper. I can't wait here all day, I get my living by the sweat of my brow, and I'm due at Seringapatam. Come, do you refuse to pay me?

Mayor. You see, my man, you grossly exaggerated the difficulty of the job. It was a mere trifle!

Piper. To *me*, yes. To *you*, no!

Mayor. I tell you what I'll do. Here's a couple of guilder. I'll give you that as drink money, and promise to recommend you to all the Mayors of my acquaintance.

Piper. Thunder and fury!   [*Chord—all start.*

Mayor. Come, don't be insolent!

Piper. I'll have my money, or—beware!

Mayor. Threatening a public functionary — the Watch there!

Piper. You'd better reflect in time. Come, *you!* Will *you* pay me?

Sauerkraut. We can't. It's a private matter between yourself and the Mayor.

Piper. Cheats! Rascals!

36

"A sweet voice calls,"

WASE

"A sweet voice calls, we must obey."

Mayor. Come, be off!

Piper. You old gourmandizing villain! Give me my money!

Mayor. If you're not out of the town in half-an-hour, I'll have you committed as a rogue and vagabond.

Liza. O, sir, I'm so sorry—it's really disgraceful.

Con. It is infamous. Look here, friend, I'm only a poor man, but there's all I have, and you're freely welcome to it.   [*Offers money.*

Piper. I don't want *your* money. I'll have revenge! But I thank you all the same, and your sweetheart. She *is* your sweetheart?

Con. Yes.

Piper. Any little sisters or brothers?

Liza. None.

Con. Why do you ask?

Piper. Oh, nothing; only my music has no effect on any human beings over fourteen years of age; but all under that age——

Liza. What do you mean?

Piper. Mischief! mischief! the pied Piper is not to be trifled with!

Trio.

Liza. O look! O look! I'm really afraid—
He foams at the mouth like a dog with rabies.

Con. It's really a shame that he hasn't been paid.

Piper. (*Fiercely.*) Now for the little boys, girls, and
    babies!

37

All that can toddle and talk and run aoout,
All that are fourteen years old and under,
All that prattle and play in the sun about !
I'll coax away, till there isn't one about—
   I will, I will, by thunder !
   [*Chord and thunder crash. All repeat, " All that
    can toddle,"* etc.

Liza. O dear ! He's now in a terrible state.
He rolls his eyes as he utters his snarlings.
 Con. His temper's bad, but his wrong is great !
 Piper. Now for the little duckies and darlings !
Dark-hair'd, golden-hair'd, sickly and healthy ones ;
The father's treasure, the mother's wonder ;
Honest and open ones, sly and stealthy ones,
Ugly and pretty, poor or wealthy ones,
   I'll have them all, by thunder !
    [*Chord and thunder crash. He rushes off.*
Liza. What can he mean ?
Con. I'm almost afraid to guess.
Liza. Oh, Conrad, I was sure he was no piper.
He's some wicked fiend.   .
 Con. What ?
 Liza. I'm sure of it ? I seemed to smell brimstone
in his very breath.
      [*Music. Cries without.*

    Enter MARTHA. *Recitative.*
 Mar. O woe ! O horror !
 Liza. Martha, what's the matter ?
      38

Mar. That terrible Piper. On his pipe he's playing,
And out of every door and every gateway
The little children flock and gladly follow !
He comes this way !

Liza. Oh, now I understand him !
Alas ! he's luring them to their destruction.

> [*Music swells. Enter the* PIPER *playing a beau-*
> *tiful melody. As he goes, swarms of little*
> *children follow behind him, of all ages up to*
> *fourteen, some lame, some blind, all looking at*
> *vacancy, and following the sound. As they sing*
> *the following, the* PIPER'S *music accompanies*
> *them, piano.*

Children. Children, children, do not stay,
      A sweet voice calls, we must obey !
      (*Voices off.*) Come away !

Children. Where the summer roses blow,
      Ripe grapes cluster, fountains flow,
      Pretty fairies white as snow,
           Come and go,
      In a bright and golden day !
           Come away.
      (*Voices.*) Come away ! come away !

Enter Citizens, *in terror.*
Chatter-Chorus.

Sight most shocking ! how they're flocking
Out of every door together.
Stop them, stay them, he will slay them !
Annchen ! Bertha ! Hans ! come hither !

Children, to PIPER's *Music.*

Hasten, hasten, do not stay !
In the golden fields we'll play,
(*Voices.*) Come away !
Children. See they beckon all in white,
Down the meadows, up the height,
In the golden summer light,
Ah, so bright !
Hasten, hasten, do not stay.
Come away !
(*Voices.*) Come away ! come away !

Recitative.

Mayor. Stop him, arrest him.   Murder ! Help !
Despair !
Piper. Back ! He who stirs a finger dies. (*Movement.*)
Beware !

Chorus.

Sight of sadness ! full of gladness
How they flock in swarms behind him !
Stop them, stay them, he will slay them !
Children ! Children ! Do not mind him.

Liza, Aria.

O hearken to our pleading and our sighing,
Spare the children, they are innocent of guile.
The houses will be empty of their crying,
And the mothers will look vainly for their smile.

"That terrible Piper.   On his pipe he's playing."

Take the strongest and the bravest of the city,
  Take the fairest, they will follow anywhere !
But spare the little children, O for pity,
  For the sake of those who love them, spare, O spare !
          Chorus. Spare them, O spare !
          Piper. Too late your prayer.
          Chorus. They're lost ! Despair!

Piper. No power can stay
          Or set them free !
          They go with me
        Far, far away !
  No more you'll hear their happy cries,
  No more you'll look into their eyes !
  Henceforth with me their souls shall dwell !
  Bid them farewell ! a last farewell!

                  Recitative.

Liza. (*To little* HANS.) Hans, is it thou ? Come
          hither, dear, come hither !
Heed not the voice that summons you away.
Alas ! he wanders on, he knows not whither,
His eyes are fixed in dream ! he will not stay

Little Hans. (*In trance.*) See ! see !
          The beautiful bright Land,
          Where the angels stand
          Beckoning and smiling to me !
          Hark, can you not hear ?
          Such sweet, sweet singing !
          And the sun shines clear,

                  41   F

Glad birds are winging,
And flowers springing.
How beautiful it seems !
And my mother's face shines bright,
Just as it does in dreams
When I lie asleep at night.

       [*Struggling in* LIZA's *arms.*
She calls, she calls, I cannot stay.
Voices. Come away ! come away !
Children. Children, children, come away,
    A sweet voice calls, we must obey.
Piper. (*In a loud voice.*) Come away !
Voices. (*Off, very piano.*) Come away ! come away !
 [*As the* Children *follow the* PIPER *up and surround*
  him, he stands towering over them in triumph,
  with a wild laugh. The people stand amazed
  and wringing their hands. To the last dying
  sound of the voices the Act-drop slowly descends.

" Hans, is it thou ?   Come hither, dear, come hither ! "

ACT II.

Sᴄᴇɴᴇ I. *The interior of the* Pɪᴘᴇʀ's *cave among the mountains.   As curtain rises the plaintive music of the intermezzo blends into opening notes of the Sleeping Chorus, and the scene, gradually revealed through a transparency, discloses groups of sleeping Children, in whose midst sits the* Pɪᴘᴇʀ *with a weird red light on him, while looking up in his face, as if fascinated, is little* Hᴀɴs. *Dim moonlight effect on children.*

Chorus of Children, sleeping.

Wᴇ are weary of straying
　　We know not whither,
To the sound of the playing
　　Which drew us hither.
It is dark and dreary
　　In these caverns deep,
But we feel so weary
　　We fain must sleep !

43

Piper.

Sleep on ! still sleep !
Be your slumbers deep !
Ye are mine to keep,
Though ye wake or sleep!

Children.

In our sleep we're dreaming
   That still we hear him !
His eyes are gleaming—
   We see and fear him !
Though he pinch and pain us,
   In vain we weep,
For he who hath ta'en us
   Still haunts our sleep.

Piper.

I haunt their sleep !
   Through their dreams I creep !
They are mine to keep,
   Though they wake or sleep !

Children.

He haunts our sleep !
   Through our dreams doth creep !
We are his to keep,
   Though we wake or sleep!

Together.

[*Music of Chorus dies away, and as the vision
   fades the scene changes to*

44

"We are weary of straying
We know not whither."

SCENE II. *Exterior of the* PIPER's *cave among the mountains, with a distant view of Hamelin seen in the faint light of dawn.*

Enter down path LIZA *and* Men *and* Women.

Chorus of Men *and* Women, *entering.*

SAD is the home where no little feet are falling,
　Dark is the hearth where no children gather round,
Far, far away, we hear them faintly calling,
　All through the night we have listen'd to the sound.
Children ! children ! come once more to bless us,
　Children ! children ! smile and come again !
Twine your arms around us, kiss us and caress us,
　Bring us back the gladness we weary for in vain.

Liza.

Look! now the Day shines o'er the mountains yonder,
　Happy and bright now the sun begins to burn,
Still far away the little children wander,
　Or sleep in the darkness, never to return !
Children ! children ! come again to bless us, etc.
　　　Chorus. Children ! children ! etc., etc.
　　　　　　　　　　　　　　　[*Sad music.*

Enter down path CONRAD.

Con. Liza, what news ?

Liza. Recitative.

None, Conrad ! All night long,
We've watch'd and listen'd, but have seen no sign.
Hither they came, lured by the Piper's playing,

45

Into the cavern, open'd to receive them,
They enter'd, and the mountain closed upon them.

[*Chorus* " Children ! children !" *repeated.*

Con. There is no hope, then ! The little ones are lost for ever ! lost and dead !

Liza. No, not dead ! All night long we have heard the faint sounds of their voices issuing from the mountain. Listen ! (*The children's voices are faintly heard in the cavern.*) They are prisoned there in a living tomb.

Con. Had your father acted like an honourable man, this calamity would never have taken place. It is all his doing. Look where he comes !

Sauerkraut. Yes, there he comes. Truly, a pretty Mayor for a city like Hamelin !

Enter MAYOR.

Men. Wretch !

Women. Cheat ! rogue ! Bring us back our children, or we will tear you limb from limb.

[*All advance upon him.*

Mayor. Help ! help !

Sauerkraut. Yes, we'll help you ! If I had my way you should be sewn up in a sack, and thrown into the river.

All. Bring us back our children !

Mayor. Give me time ! I admit my fault, but I did not suspect I was dealing with a fiend.

[*Low subterranean thunder, and laughter off. All shrink away in terror.*

46

Mayor. Help! help!　　　　　　*[Falls on his knees.*

Con. Silence! There is but one way to save the little ones. In the name of the whole city, you must interview this mysterious being, and offer him compensation.

Mayor. *I* interview him! All the saints forbid.
　　　　　　　　　　　　　　　　　[Going.

Men. *(Seizing him).* Stay!

Con. What, are you afraid? Then, by heaven, I'll do it.

Mayor. Do! and if you succeed, you shall have my blessing and my daughter into the bargain.

Con. That you promise?

Mayor. That I promise.

　　　[Laughter off repeated. All shrinking and crying.

Con. Cowards, what is there to fear? If this being is the very Prince of Evil himself, I'll confront him. *(Going up and knocking at rock.)* Within there!

Voice. *(Within.)* Who knocks?

Con. I, Conrad the Cooper, of Hamelin!

Voice. What seek you?

Con. The wretch who robbed the city of its children! The evil spirit who has made our homes desolate.

Voice. Beware!　　　　　　　　*[Low thunder.*

Liza. *(Rushing to* CONRAD.*)* Conrad! come back! he will destroy you!

Con. *(Embracing her.)* Hush, dearest. Let him destroy me if he wills! What is my life worth compared to the happiness of a whole city? *(Knocking*

47

again). Within there, I say! Man, spirit, devil—whatever you are—answer and come forth!

> [*Crash and chord. The* PIPER *appears on the threshold of the cavern. All shrink back crying but* CONRAD *and* LIZA, *who embrace and stand facing him.*

Piper. (*Smiling diabolically*). Good morning!

Mayor. Liza, my child, come hither.

Piper. Who speaks? The wretch who broke his word and refused me the wages I had fairly earned!

Mayor. Sir, on my honour.

Piper. Your honour? The honour of a Mayor! Swindler, for all that has taken place, you only are to blame.

Sauerkraut. He is, the scoundrel!

All. He is! He is! The villain!

> [*Threatening* MAYOR.

Piper. Then why don't you throw him after the rats into the river Weser? [*They groan.*

Sauerkraut. Do you hear that? Come, friends, let's make a job of it.

All. We will! we will!

Mayor. No! no! Help! Mercy! (*Falls on his knees*). Liza, plead for me. Tell them I repent.

Piper. Too late!

Women. Give us back our children, and this old man shall be punished as he deserves.

Sauerkraut. Yes, we'll look after that. Give us back the little ones, and we'll soon polish off the Mayor.

48

All. We will.

Piper. No ; a bargain's a bargain. I shall keep the little ones, unless——

Con. Unless——

Piper. Unless (*looking at* Liza) the Mayor can offer me a *quid pro quo.*

Mayor. Anything—everything—except myself.

Piper. Ha ha! I want something infinitely younger and more charming. The fact is, I'm looking for a *wife.* [*Laughter off.*

Mayor. A wife? Is that all? You shall have a *thousand.*

Piper. Thanks! One's good enough for me. Bring me an acceptable bride, and you shall have back your brats! But mind, I'm very particular. The wife I want must be a perfect maiden—pretty, of course— young and good-tempered, a first-rate cook, a good needlewoman—in short, a paragon !

[*Crash. He vanishes.*

Con. You hear ?

A Woman. Of course we hear ; but it's out of the question.

Con. Will no one volunteer ? It will only be one woman the less, and the little ones will be saved.

A very ugly old Crone. Well, I haven't long to live, and if the gentleman really wants to marry——

[*All laugh.*

Con. Absurd ! You're seventy, if you're a day ! Come, girls, won't one of you save the city ? Annchen, what do you say ?

Annchen. I'd rather drown myself than marry a monster like that!

Girls. And I! and I!

A Man. Besides, they've all got sweethearts.

Girls. Yes, yes!

Con. So you all refuse?

Girls. Of course we do.

A Girl. If you're so anxious to save the children, why don't you offer him your *own* sweetheart?

Con. My Liza! Heaven forbid! (*To* LIZA, *who has sunk on stone, hiding her face.*) Courage, dearest! There is nothing to fear! I will speak to this demon again, and—— [*Going up.*

Mayor. Stay, one moment! Will you leave this little affair to me?

Con. No, no; we've had enough of your meddling!

Sauerkraut. Yes, we've done with you till we put you in that sack.

Mayor. But suppose I can get you out of the difficulty? I always had a winning way with ladies. (*Goes to* 1st *Girl.*) Now look here, my dear, a man of that kind often makes a good husband, and he's very musical.

1st Girl. Thank you, I don't care about that sort of music.

Mayor. Then you, my love. (*Addressing another.*) They tell me he's got a beautiful place in Seringapatam.

2nd Girl. I prefer to stay in Hamelin.

Mayor. (*Going to another.*) What do you say, dear?

You're not so young as you were, and it's a great
thing to be comfortably settled.

3rd Girl. Go away, or I'll scratch you!

Crash. The PIPER *reappears.*

Piper. Well, what have you decided?

Con. Nothing; no girl in her senses would marry you!

Piper. What is the objeɛtion? I am not exaɛtly beautiful, but I have pleasant manners; and, above all, I am rich. If you really want the children back——

Women. Yes, yes—give us our children!

Piper. Not till you bring me a bride of whom I approve.

Mayor. My dear sir, you may choose for yourself. We have a large assortment of every kind of bride on hand. May I recommend you this one, warranted to wear beautifully? [*Leads forward one of the women.*

Piper. Take her away! She's too fat!

Mayor. Here is another, less open to that objeɛtion.

Piper. Pshaw! a broomstick!

Mayor. Then what do you say to *this* charming person?

Piper. Humph! not so bad. Step forward, young woman. Have you ever been married before?

Mayor. (*Whispering.*) Say "never."

Girl. Never!

Piper. Let me look at you. (*Laughs.*) Ha, ha, ha! Why, you've had *two* husbands, and one of them,

poor wretch, is still alive. (Girl *screams and runs away*.)
At your tricks again, Mayor! Don't try to impose
on *me!*

Girl. (*To other* Girls, *aside*.) I don't care. I'm not
afraid. (*Stepping forward*.) If you really want to get
married——

Piper. I do. What's your name?

Girl. Deborah.

Piper. Can you sew?

Girl. Yes.

Piper. And cook?

Girl. Plain cooking.

Piper. Amiable?

Girl. (*Tossing head*.) Oh, *very!*   [*Laugh.*

Piper. (*Laughing*.) Ha, ha, ha! Deborah Meerschaum, the greatest slattern and the sharpest shrew in
Hamelin! Away with you! You won't suit *me!*

Girl. (*Tossing her head and retiring*.) Well, I'm
sure!

Mayor. My dear sir, you're very difficult to please!

Piper. I am. Listen, and you shall hear the sort of
wife I want.

Piper's Song.

I.

I want to marry, if you please,
    If you please, if you please;
And night and day my fancy sees
    The maid I mean to marry!

52

I hate your widows, fat and round,
Waddling like geese upon the ground,
Though they in beauty may abound,
    They've too much flesh to carry ! . . .
I'll have a bride that's not too thin,
    Not too fat, not too thin ;
With clear bright eyes and dimpled chin
    And cheeks where roses tarry.
No slut and slattern, with her shoe
Down at the heel, will ever do !
And from a snapping, scolding shrew
    Heaven save me, when I marry !

II.

I want to marry, if you please,
    If you please, if you please ;
But no ill-temper'd sulking tease
    Will ever make me marry !
Your prude, moreover, I despise,
Who walks along with downcast eyes,
Blushes and simpers, smirks and sighs—
    May all her arts miscarry !
My bride must not be over shy,
    Not too bold, not too shy ;
Though from her tender eyes must fly
    Love's shafts, which few can parry !
Nor must she be a maiden pert,
With tossing head and flouncing skirt—
Of all the sex I loathe a flirt,
    And such I'll never marry !

53

Piper. Nothing but perfection will content me. And besides, between ourselves, I've taken a fancy. Give me *your own daughter*, and it's a bargain.

Liza. (*Springing up.*) Me? O Conrad!

Con. Fear not, Liza.

Mayor. My good man, what you ask is impossible! My daughter is *engaged!*

Piper. To Conrad the Cooper, to whom you yourself have shown the door? Be it so. You've heard my ultimatum. Either I marry your daughter, or the children remain with me for ever.

All. Mercy! mercy!

Piper. And remember, not one of them will be able to escape me. I can tease them and weary them, pinch them black and blue, feed them on black bread and cold water, or starve them altogether; send spiders, rats, and daddy-longlegs to frighten them, and make them study such hard lessons that they'll cry their eyes out. If you refuse me your daughter's hand the children will be mine for ever!

All. Mercy! mercy!

Piper. My mind's made up. It remains for the old man and the girl herself to decide. And observe: I won't take her without a dowry, and that dowry must be the one thousand guilders of which you robbed me yesterday.

Children's Chorus, off.

Father, mother, we are weary,
   All the golden light has fled ;
In the dark it is so dreary,
   And the cold earth is our bed.

Piper. You hear ? They call as from the grave,
   'Tis yours to slay them or to save.

First Chorus, repeated.

Children, children, come once more to bless us !
Children, children, come once more again !

Children, off.

Father, mother, kiss us and caress us,
   Take us back, nor let us plead and cry in vain !

Piper. For the last time, decide. You refuse ? Then——
Liza. (*With a cry.*) Stay, I will consent !
Con. No, no, you *shall* not !
Liza. I *must.* What you said was true. It will be only one woman the less, and the little ones will be spared. (*To* PIPER.) I am ready ; take *me*, I will be yours !
Piper. Agreed. What say you, Mayor ?
Mayor. (*Trembling.*) If my daughter is willing——
Piper. You've heard her say so. Now, away with you ! Fetch the dowry—good sound golden guilders,

55

mind, no paper money—and we'll arrange the whole affair without delay.

[*Points* MAYOR *off. Music. People flock off with* MAYOR. CONRAD *and* LIZA *remain. The* PIPER *looks at them one moment, while* CONRAD *makes an appealing gesture, then, with a laugh, vanishes into cavern.*

Con. Liza, my darling, reflect! Think of the love I bear you! do not break my heart.

[*Faint chorus of* Children, *repeated off, through her answer.*

Liza. Think of *them!* Think of the little ones whom he has taken away. Listen, they are crying; and *I* can save them! Yes, I will give my life for theirs!

Con. And I—what shall I do?

Liza. Comfort yourself with the thought that I died for *them.*

Con. No, no! I cannot bear it! Liza, stay with me!

Duet. Conrad and Liza.

I.

He. I cannot part from thee, my darling,
 Till life's last breath hath pass'd away.
She. Too late—our dream of joy is over—
 He calls me hence—I cannot stay.
He. A silken thread of Love's own twining
 Links us together, heart to heart—
My heart will break if *that* is broken!
 Light of my life, we must not part.

56

By a golden brook.

"I bathed my feet in the waters sweet."

He. I cannot part from thee, my darling,
  Till life's last breath hath pass'd away.
Heed not the voice which calls thee from
    me,
Hark to the voice which whispers "stay!"
She. Yes, I must part from thee, my
    darling,
  My bridegroom beckons me away—
Our Summer dream of joy is over—
  He calls me hence! I cannot stay!

} *Together.*

II.

She. He calls me hence—I have sworn   go—
  Though I shrink and cry in pain ;
Forget not, dear, that I loved thee so,
  Though I never return again!
He. By the vows we plighted so long ago,
  By the dream we dream'd in vain,
By the heart that breaks to lose thee so,
  Light of my life, remain !
      Oh!
He. I cannot part from thee, my darling,
    etc.
She. Yes, I must part from thee, my
    darling, etc.

} *Together.*

  [*At the end of song* LIZA *sinks half kneeling, half
    fainting, at the mouth of cavern, while* CONRAD
    stands despairing, R. *The* PIPER *appears.*

57   H

Piper. Well, is my bride prepared?

Liza. (*Sobbing.*)   Yes, I am ready.

Piper. One kiss, then, on the lips, to seal the
    bargain.

Con. (*Drawing sword.*) Forbear to touch her, or this
    sword shall slay thee.

Piper. (*Uplifting hands.*) Do *thou* forbear, young
    man, to cross thy master.

> [CONRAD'S *sword falls from his grasp. The* PIPER
> *lifts* LIZA *gently, and leads her down, singing*
> *softly.*

Here are lips as red as roses,
    Eyes of tender violet blue;
Where this pretty head reposes
    Youth should shine in brightest hue!
Tell me, child, if I should wed thee,
    Wouldst thou tremble and repine?

Liza. Yes, I shrink from thee and dread thee,
    Yet, for *their* sakes, I'll be thine.   [*Repeat.*

Con. Yes, her very soul doth dread
    thee,
    Though, for *their* sakes, she'll
    be thine.   } *Together.*
Piper. Yes, her very soul doth dread
    me,
    Though, for duty's sake, she's
    mine.

Piper. Then you do not hesitate, though misery may be your lot ?

Liza. No, no ! Restore the little children, and I consent.

Piper. (*Patting her head.*) Courage, my child ! Perhaps the Pied Piper is not so black as he is painted. (*To* CONRAD.) As for you, young man, I owe you an obligation. When the rogue of a Mayor cheated me of my due, you alone offered to act like an honest man. What can I do for you in return ?

Con. Kill me ! Put me out of my misery for ever !

Piper. (*Laughs.*) Ha, ha, ha ! Wait a little, and we shall see. First, let me inspect my bride's dowry, which they are bringing me from the city.

· *Enter* Girls *and* Men, MAYOR *and* Citizens,
with Men *carrying bags of money.*

Chatter-Chorus.

Sight of pity ! from the city
  Come they with their golden dower,
While the maiden, terror laden,
  Mourns her bitter bridal hour.
See ! he smiles with fiendish pleasure
  On both money-bags and bride,
Yet he keeps a richer treasure
  In the gloomy mountain side.

[*During Chorus the* Men *lay money-bags at the* PIPER'S *feet.*

59

Piper. Is the gold all there ?

Mayor. It is, most worshipful sir.

Piper. A thousand guilders.

Mayor. (*Bows.*)

Piper. If there be but the weight of one single groschen missing, look to yourself.

Mayor. On my honour.

Piper. *Your* honour! Then the bargain is complete?

Mayor. Excuse me, on *our* side, not on *yours.*

Piper. Ha! you doubt me ?

Mayor. (*Recoiling.*) By no means—only in matters of business——

Piper. Enough ! I'll keep my word. Attend !

[*Music. He plays on pipe. The* Children's *voices are heard coming nearer and nearer, growing more and more joyful.*

Children.

Father, mother, we are waking !
  Brightly shine the morning beams,
Overhead the clouds are breaking,
  And we rise from happy dreams.
Fast through flowery garden closes
  Sparkling bright with golden dew,
Up glad pathways strewn with roses,
  We are hastening back to *you !*
Running after, with sweet laughter,
  Pretty fays sing loud and clear ;

60

" Merry cries and rippling laughter
  Greet him as he dances round ! "

Homeward straying, gladly playing,
  Bright and happy, we are *here !*

[*At end of Chorus the Cavern opens in a flood of
  light, and the* Children, *carrying flowers and
  garlands, trip on to the stage, and run to their
  kinsfolk. General happiness and embracing.*

Recitative.

Hans. (*Lame boy of Act I., but without crutches.*)

  Look, Liza, look !   [*Shows flowers.*
  By a golden brook
I found them growing, in the summer sun,
  And I bathed my feet
  In the waters sweet,
And was lame no more, but could leap and run !
                    [*Leaps into her arms.*

Chorus of Children.

  Father, mother, we are waking !
    Brightly shine the morning beams,
  Overhead the clouds are breaking,
    And we wake from happy dreams.

Recitative.

Liza. Alas ! alas !   [*Sinks on bank, hiding her face.*
Hans.   O Liza, you are weeping !
And we are all so glad ; what is it, dear ?
  Liza. 'Tis like the hand of Death upon me
    creeping.
Look, look, he beckons, and I shrink in fear !

61

Piper. Is the bride ready ?

All. The bride is ready !

Piper. (*To* MAYOR.) And is this her marriage portion ?   [*Points to money-bags.*

Mayor. (*Trembling.*) This is her marriage portion !

Piper. (*Taking* LIZA's *hand.*) Upon your head,
    child, may all blessings shower. (*To* CONRAD.)
Embrace the bride ! she's *yours*—and there's her
    Dower !
I only tried your hearts with sore affliction,
To prove them true, and bring them benediction !
    [*With a cry of joy* CONRAD *and* LIZA *spring into
    each other's arms.*

Piper. (*Smiling and beckoning to* Children.) Laugh,
    little ones, in merry acclamation !
And ring, ye bells, to swell the jubilation !
    [Children *surround him joyfully.*   *General Chorus
    and valediction of* PIPER *up to finale and
    general picture.*

Piper. So now you know that I'm not so low and
    spiteful as other pipers !
Though the tunes I play bring much dismay to wicked
    people and vipers !
I tune my mirth to the joy of Earth and love the little
    ones rarely—
The Piper, in short, is a decent sort of a fellow when
    treated fairly !

Chorus. The Piper, in short, etc.
           [Children *laugh and clap hands.*

62

Con.   May a thousand blessings be
    On thy music and on thee !
Liza. May our children's children bless
    All thy love and gentleness !
      Chorus. May our children's children, etc.

      Conrad, Liza, and Chorus.

Happy maidens and true lovers
    Faery music ne'er makes sad ;
Where the magic Piper hovers
    Little children shall be glad.
[*During above the* PIPER *dances round stage while
the* Children *follow, laughing and clapping
hands. Bells ring in distance to final Chorus.*

Children. Children, children, follow after,
    Where he flies with leap and bound ;
Merry cries and rippling laughter
    Greet him as he dances round !

Piper. Ha, ha, ha !
Children. (*Clapping hands.*) Ha, ha, ha !
Piper. (*Going up stage.*) Good luck ! good-bye !
All. Good luck ! good-bye !

Piper.   Though afar I now must wander,
    Up the hills and o'er the streams,
From the Faery Land up yonder
    Still I'll send you happy dreams !
        63

Children. Think of *us* where'er you wander,
　　　Up the hills and o'er the streams,
　　From the Faery Land up yonder
　　　Send us more such happy dreams !

[PIPER *waves hand and vanishes to chord.* Children *wave hands, embraced by their friends.*
CONRAD *and* LIZA *embrace,* c. *To the
sound of laughter and merriment and ringing
bells the curtain falls.*

CURTAIN.

www.ingramcontent.com/pod-product-compliance
Lightning Source LLC
Chambersburg PA
CBHW022009050726
47499CB00008BA/2733